LIFE IN THE SPECIAL FORCES

LIFE AS AN
ARMY RANGER

by Sue Bradford Edwards

BrightP✦int Press

San Diego, CA

© 2024 BrightPoint Press
an imprint of ReferencePoint Press, Inc.
Printed in the United States

For more information, contact:
BrightPoint Press
PO Box 27779
San Diego, CA 92198
www.BrightPointPress.com

ALL RIGHTS RESERVED.

No part of this work covered by the copyright hereon may be reproduced or used in any form or by any means—graphic, electronic, or mechanical, including photocopying, recording, taping, web distribution, or information storage retrieval systems—without the written permission of the publisher.

LIBRARY OF CONGRESS CATALOGING-IN-PUBLICATION DATA

Names: Edwards, Sue Bradford, author.
Title: Life as an Army Ranger / by Sue Bradford Edwards.
Description: San Diego, CA: ReferencePoint Press, Inc., 2024 | Series: Life in the Special
  Forces | Audience: Grade 7 to 9 | Includes bibliographical references and index.
Identifiers: ISBN 9781678207465 (hardcover) | ISBN 9781678207472 (eBook)
The complete Library of Congress record is available at www.loc.gov.

CONTENTS

AT A GLANCE	4
INTRODUCTION	6
LEADING THE WAY	
CHAPTER ONE	12
BECOMING AN ARMY RANGER	
CHAPTER TWO	24
ARMY RANGER EQUIPMENT	
CHAPTER THREE	34
THE WORK OF ARMY RANGERS	
CHAPTER FOUR	44
ARMY RANGER MISSIONS	
Glossary	58
Source Notes	59
For Further Research	60
Index	62
Image Credits	63
About the Author	64

AT A GLANCE

- US Army Rangers are one of several special forces groups in the US military.

- The standards for becoming a Ranger are very high. Only about 50 percent of people who begin training graduate.

- Army Rangers often fly to their missions in Chinook or Little Bird helicopters. They parachute or slide down a rope to the ground.

- The weapons used by many Rangers are M4A1 carbines and Glock 17 or Glock 19 handguns.

- Airborne Rangers specialize in parachute jumps. But some Rangers dive or climb mountains.

- Army Rangers train for many jobs. Some Rangers handle communications while others treat the injured.

- One of the best-known Ranger missions was Operation Red Wings in 2005. Rangers aided injured Navy SEAL Marcus Luttrell in Afghanistan.

- Not all Army Ranger missions involve combat. Rangers also gather information and carry out rescues.

INTRODUCTION

LEADING THE WAY

It was a dark night in 2015. Sergeant 1st Class Thomas "Patrick" Payne and his team scaled a prison wall. The US Army Rangers and local allies came to the prison in northern Iraq on a mission. The soldiers wore night-vision goggles. But it was still hard to see. Terrorists inside the prison had opened fire. Dust and smoke clouded the air. The team split in half. Each group would clear one of the two prison buildings. A terrorist group called the Islamic State of Iraq and Syria (ISIS) was holding **hostages** in the buildings.

Payne's team cleared ISIS fighters who guarded one building. The team used bolt cutters to open locks on the prison doors.

Army Rangers spend extensive time training with equipment such as night-vision devices to help ensure success when they use the technology on missions.

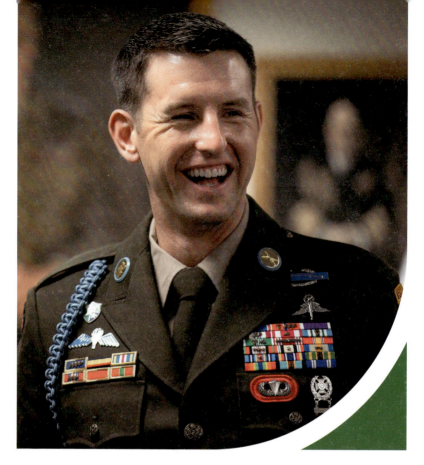

The United States honored Payne for his brave actions in the hostage rescue in Iraq. President Donald Trump awarded the Army Ranger the Medal of Honor on September 11, 2020.

Payne's crew led thirty-eight hostages to safety.

The second team was still battling ISIS fighters. Members of the team radioed for help to free the other hostages. The building had caught fire.

Payne and his team headed to the second building. They climbed a ladder onto the roof. But before they found a way inside, bombs went off. ISIS fighters had blown up their suicide vests. The blasts shook the building. Payne led his team back to the ground.

They took cover. Payne could see two locks on the building's doors. He ran through gunfire holding bolt cutters. He used them to cut the first lock. But the building was still on fire. Smoke forced him to retreat. An Iraqi ally worked at the second lock. Smoke also forced him back. Payne returned and finished cutting the second lock. More than thirty hostages emerged. Payne reentered the burning building. He led the last hostage outside before the building collapsed.

Rangers led the hostages to the landing site amid gunfire. Payne got everyone on board the helicopters. To make enough room, his team stood. They flew everyone to safety. In 2020, Payne met President Donald Trump. The president gave Payne the Medal of Honor.

WHO ARE THE ARMY RANGERS?

US Army Rangers are an elite force. The Ranger motto is "Rangers Lead the Way." They often head into danger. Their missions take place all over the world. On many missions, they capture or kill terrorists. They also rescue soldiers or civilians. Civilians are people who are not members of the military.

Some Army Ranger missions require a small team. Others require many soldiers.

Sliding down ropes from helicopters allows special forces members to deploy quickly to the ground.

Rangers work hard to ensure mission success. They parachute in or slide down ropes from helicopters. Rangers climb mountains and hike long distances. Sometimes they cross water using small boats. Army Rangers train to be ready at a moment's notice.

1
BECOMING AN ARMY RANGER

To become an Army Ranger, a person must join the US Army. The first step is to take the Armed Services Vocational Aptitude Battery (ASVAB). This series of tests can be taken any time during the school year. But many high schools schedule it each spring and fall.

The test is split into several areas. They include math, reading, science, electronics, mechanics, and putting objects together. How well someone scores in each area shows their strengths and weaknesses.

ASVAB scores help decide what job the Army gives each person. A Ranger

Soldiers who want to become Army Rangers can retake the ASVAB if they didn't earn high enough scores the first time. The Army even offers classes to help them prepare.

candidate must have a high skilled tech score. This combined score includes math, reading, science, mechanics, and vocabulary.

To start Ranger training, soldiers must be 17 to 34 years old. They need a high school or general educational development (GED) diploma. They must also be US citizens.

Ranger candidates must be extremely fit. Everyone in the Army must pass a fitness test. But Ranger applicants must earn especially high scores. Rangers are required to perform fifty-three push-ups in 2 minutes. They then have to do fifty-nine sit-ups in 2 minutes. These tests are followed by a 2-mile (3.2-km) run that Rangers need to finish in less than 14.5 minutes. Afterward, they do four pull-ups. Finally, they must carry a 35-pound (15.9-kg) pack and

The standards of physical fitness are higher for Army Rangers than for other members of this military branch.

a weapon. And with all this weight, they must hike 6 miles (9.7 km) in less than 90 minutes.

The dangerous nature of Army Ranger missions makes it especially important that these special forces members can count on one another when it matters most.

THE TRAITS OF ARMY RANGERS

Army Ranger missions are among the hardest in the military. Rangers gather information in enemy territory. They conduct raids and perform rescues. Doing these things places Rangers in danger. Former Ranger Jesse Gould says, "An Army Ranger embodies the rare individual that runs toward danger and difficulty."[1]

Army Rangers often find themselves in life-or-death situations. They must think fast in difficult circumstances. This can mean developing a new plan of attack. It can also mean finding a new route when cut off by enemy forces. It can even mean carrying on when a fellow Ranger is killed.

Each ranger must rely on his or her own training. Still, Rangers work as a team. "A Ranger is a team player, leaves no one behind, and shares what he has," says former Ranger Dave Eubank.[2] To succeed, Rangers must know that other Rangers have their backs.

TRAINING TO BECOME AN ARMY RANGER

Ranger training is designed to be difficult. It pushes candidates physically and mentally. People from any branch of the military can go through Ranger training. There are three phases to this training.

Phase One is often called Moore Phase. It takes place at Fort Moore in Georgia. In the first week, candidates learn to use maps, a compass, and other tools. This equipment helps the soldiers find their way through unfamiliar countryside. Soldiers must march 12 miles (19.3 km) carrying a 35-pound (15.9-kg) pack. They are given no drinking water for this exercise.

Only two-thirds of candidates make it to the second part of Moore Phase.

US ARMY RANGER BASES

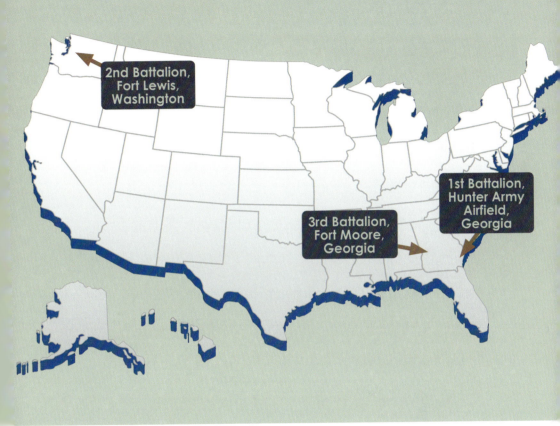

Army Rangers are divided into three battalions. Each one can be sent anywhere in the world with 18 hours' notice.

In this part, soldiers learn to capture and control an area. They learn demolition. This means destroying objects with explosives. Soldiers take part in battle drills. They must also complete the Darby Queen obstacle course. This 1-mile (1.6-km) course includes twenty obstacles. Candidates scale walls, climb ropes and cargo nets, and run across logs. Some Rangers learn to parachute during the second part of Moore Phase.

Phase Two is Mountain Phase. It takes place in northern Georgia. Candidates learn to move through mountain terrain. They also learn knot tying, climbing, and **rappelling**. One rappel that measures 200 feet (61 m) takes place at night. Soldiers learn to capture an airfield and rescue captives. They practice leading other soldiers.

Phase Three is Swamp Phase. It is at Florida's Eglin Air Force Base. Soldiers travel by boat and build rope bridges to cross rivers. "Minimal food and that sleep deprivation puts a stress on every

Soldiers training to become Army Rangers rappel down a cliff face of Yonah Mountain in Georgia. Their goal is to reach the ground as quickly as possible.

individual," says Lisa Jaster. She was the third woman to finish Ranger training. "Everybody thinks about quitting."[3] People who complete training earn their Ranger tab. This is a patch on their uniform that says "Ranger."

People in other military branches can join the Army to become Rangers. But they need more training. They join other Army members in the Ranger Assessment and Selection Program (RASP). Everyone in this

HOW MANY SUCCEED?

Each year, about 4,000 soldiers enroll in Ranger training. Only about half of them graduate. RASP is even harder. Less than half of enlisted soldiers complete it. Officers attend a different version of RASP. Just over one-quarter of them complete it.

program is assessed in **marksmanship**, medical training, and combat tactics. Candidates who complete this program can wear the tan Ranger beret. They also earn their Ranger scroll. This patch says "75th Ranger Rgt." These people are assigned to the 1st, 2nd, or 3rd Battalion in the Army's 75th Ranger Regiment. This is the special forces group known as the Army Rangers.

2
ARMY RANGER EQUIPMENT

Army Rangers need many types of equipment. This includes vehicles. Rangers use helicopters to travel long distances. The massive Chinook helicopter has two rotors for maximum lift. It can haul heavy cargo. The Black Hawk is a medium-sized helicopter. It is rugged and dependable. Rangers **fast rope** from this aircraft to the ground. The smaller Little Bird carries only six Rangers. They sit on two benches on the outside of the helicopter.

Rangers also use Land Rovers. This vehicle's turbocharged diesel engine powers it rapidly down the road. The Land Rover is big enough for several Rangers

Army Rangers use helicopters such as the Black Hawk to reach their missions. They may fast rope or parachute to the ground.

and their gear. Machine guns and grenade launchers can be mounted on the outside of Land Rovers. Some Land Rovers can carry stretchers to move the wounded. Land Rovers can be carried in Chinook helicopters. Chinooks can also carry Land Rovers in slings. The sling hangs beneath the helicopter.

ARMY RANGER WEAPONS

Army Rangers are trained to use many different weapons. Many Rangers carry a Glock 19 handgun. This gun weighs only 1.4 pounds (0.6 kg). This is lighter than the M9 Beretta handgun that many other members of the military carry. Rangers must often carry 75 pounds (34 kg) of gear. They cut weight wherever possible.

Since many Army Rangers' missions must be performed in darkness, night-vision goggles are an essential piece of equipment for these special forces members.

Handguns work best for close combat. Rangers carry the M4A1 carbine to shoot from far away. Smaller than a rifle, it weighs only 6.5 pounds (2.9 kg). Soldiers can add **infrared** lasers, flashlights, and sights to the carbine. The Ranger aims by looking through the sight.

27

Rangers also use specialty weapons. Sniper rifles allow a shooter to hit a distant target. One sniper rifle is the MK 12 Mod 1 SPR. This variant of the M16 rifle has a range of 2,300 feet (700 m). Other options include shoulder-fired missiles. The FIM-92 Stinger can bring down an enemy aircraft. The FGM-148 Javelin is used against armored vehicles. Both missiles are heat seeking. This means they find and target the heat from an engine. Once fired, they do not need to be steered. They guide themselves to the target. The Army calls this a fire-and-forget system.

KIT BAG AND WAR BELT

Each Army Ranger keeps basic gear in a kit bag. This way, Rangers can leave quickly for

The FIM-92 Stinger can hit targets as far away as 5 miles (8 km).

their missions. The kit bag always contains the Ranger's **ballistic** helmet. This item shields the Ranger from **shrapnel**. It also has other gear mounted to it. Night-vision goggles amplify light. They enable Rangers to see even on a moonless night.

An Army Ranger's equipment includes some advanced technology. But some vital items are among the simplest, such as a compass.

The helmet also holds Peltor earmuffs. They plug into communication equipment. "These essentially give me the ability to communicate calmly with my team and it protects my ears from loud noises when we are shooting our weapons or conducting breaches," says Sgt. 1st Class Jacob Braun.[4]

On the back of the helmet are two more items. A battery pack powers the night-vision goggles. An infrared strobe shows as a flashing light in the other Rangers' night-vision goggles. It helps the Rangers keep track of each other in dark conditions.

The kit bag also carries the Ranger's plate carrier. This vest holds armor plates. They shield the Ranger from gunfire. Rangers also carry a cell phone with global positioning system (GPS) features. This helps Rangers find their mission sites. It also shows military leaders the Ranger team's location. Other gear includes extra ammunition, a headlamp, and a compass.

Like the GPS, the compass can be used to navigate. Rangers also carry extra batteries and first aid supplies.

Army Rangers wear a war belt over their uniform. It attaches to the belt they use on their pants. One of the most important items on the war belt is the airframe tether. It connects the Ranger to an aircraft. With it fastened, the Ranger cannot fall from the aircraft.

RANGER HANDBOOK

Modern communications and weapons enable Rangers to do their jobs better. A modern handbook is also important. In 2021, the Army created a digital Ranger handbook. This allows Rangers to find information even more quickly. They can also more easily review tactics before planning an operation.

All Rangers also carry extra fast rope gloves. "Every Ranger will keep a pair of those typically rubber banded to their kit or to their belt," says Braun.[5] If a helicopter cannot land, the team may have to fast rope. Gloves must be worn. Without them, the rope would tear the Ranger's hands. An injury such as that could keep the Ranger from doing his or her job.

3

THE WORK OF ARMY RANGERS

Any soldier who has completed basic training can apply to Army Ranger School. Enlisted troops attend the full Army Ranger School. Officers attend a special school. The Army wants only the best officers to lead Rangers.

Officers study Ranger tactics. They also plan Ranger missions. When a plan must be changed, officers create new plans.

They must think fast and communicate the new plans well. Officers must coordinate other Rangers. Soldiers of every rank are needed for Ranger missions to succeed.

The first twenty days of Army Ranger School are designed to prepare a soldier's body and mind for the rest of the training experience. The soldiers need both physical and mental strength to succeed.

APPLYING THEIR SKILLS

All Army Rangers train to scout, collect information, and fight. But Rangers can also train in other areas. These areas are chosen to make the best use of each Ranger's individual skills. Rangers who are good with technology may train to be communicators. They work with satellites, computers, and radios.

Army Rangers who are good with technology may also work with drones. Drones are small aircraft that soldiers operate remotely. Drones carry cameras. They enable Rangers to gather information about their surroundings. They show wooded areas and roads. Drone cameras also help Rangers spot their targets. Rangers sometimes use RQ-28A drones.

Quadcopter drones can perform vertical takeoffs and landings. These features make it possible for Army Rangers to use these drones almost anywhere.

These drones are quadcopters with four rotors. They can be folded into a backpack. It takes time for drone operators to learn to use the controls. With skill, operators can make the drones land, take off, and hover. They can also make the drone perch, sitting on a roof or in a tree. Rangers who are

Combat engineers take cover as they learn how to blast through barriers during breaching training.

good at fixing things may be assigned to repair drones.

Combat engineers are problem solvers. They find solutions when an obstacle stands between Rangers and their mission. Combat engineers build bridges and blast through walls. They flatten barbed wire barriers. They also create obstacles to block the enemy.

    The list of jobs Rangers can do is long. Rangers trained in medicine treat injuries. Some Rangers are builders. They learn to work with power tools. They develop masonry and carpentry skills. Other Rangers collect information about the enemy. Because Rangers use computers, some Rangers must keep their computer networks safe from hackers. Other Rangers know foreign languages. They translate and summarize messages. Some Ranger officers specialize in weapons systems. They study tactics to use with cannons, missiles, and rockets.

MOVING ON

Some Rangers may seek out new roles within that special force. They can train for specialties. These include airborne, mountain climbing, and diving. Rangers who go to officer training school can become officers. They then lead their fellow rangers. Once they have been officers for several years, they can become Ranger instructors.

Army captain Thomas R. Church is a Ranger instructor. He says, "An instructor must be Airborne and Ranger qualified and be a staff sergeant or above."[6] Instructors must be trained in six specialties. They must be qualified as parachute jumpmasters, mountaineers, and assault climbers. Instructors must also be qualified

Instructors must be ready to demonstrate important skills. For example, Army Rangers in training learn how to rappel by watching instructors perform the task.

as pathfinders. These are people who

are dropped in to create and manage a

drop zone. Instructors must be trained divers and combat lifesavers.

This varied experience is vital. It helps instructors see the value of Ranger training. "During my last deployment to Afghanistan with the 10th Mountain Division, I had been tested many times where I had to draw upon my Ranger training," says Church. "It helped me stay calm under fire and assisted

JUMP!

Airborne Rangers begin their training on the ground. They progress to the jump towers. Many of the towers are 250 feet (76 m) tall. Rangers in training parachute from the tower. They practice landing without getting hurt. In the next phase, they parachute from an airplane. Airborne-qualified Rangers wear the Jump Wings pin.

me in bringing my soldiers back home to their families."[7]

Army Rangers can retire after 20 years. But the longer they serve, the more money they earn in retirement. This income is called a pension.

When Rangers retire, they can use their Ranger training in new ways. Some start their own companies. They might provide security or teach people military tactics. Other retired Rangers work with veterans. This can include helping people with **post-traumatic stress disorder**. As skilled leaders, they may run for office. Some retired Rangers keep pushing themselves physically. They may compete in athletic events like ultramarathons. An ultramarathon is longer than a marathon. It is any race longer than 26.2 miles (42.2 km).

4
ARMY RANGER MISSIONS

On June 28, 2005, four US Navy SEALs were on a mission called Operation Red Wings. They were scouting for terrorist Ahmad Shah in Afghanistan. Shah was a Taliban ally. The Taliban is a radical political and religious group. The group punishes people who are US allies.

Local people saw the SEAL team. Shortly after this, the team was attacked by about fifty Taliban fighters. All four SEALs were soon wounded. They radioed for help.

Helicopters moved toward the SEALs. A Chinook carried eight SEALs and eight other Army special forces troops. Before it could reach the injured SEALs, the

A rocket-propelled grenade is a popular weapon for terrorists. US special forces are also trained to use this type of weapon.

helicopter was hit with a rocket-propelled grenade. The aircraft crashed.

The four wounded SEALs were almost out of ammunition. But they continued to fight as long as possible. Hospital Corpsman 2nd Class Marcus Luttrell was knocked out. His companions died.

When Rangers from the 2nd Battalion reached the crash site, they were discouraged. It appeared that everyone aboard the Chinook had been killed. They believed the original four SEALs were dead as well. But then a message came. Luttrell had walked 7 miles (11.3 km) from the attack site. Local people were hiding him. The Rangers climbed down the mountain. They found Luttrell injured but alive.

"When I first saw him, I picked him up," said former Ranger Mario Reyes. "I guess

Army Rangers rescued Luttrell (third from right) after he survived an attack that killed the other SEALs on the Operation Red Wings mission.

that's one of the proudest moments in my military career, because I know that there's at least one American that's alive because of what I've done."[8] Reyes and his fellow Rangers escorted Luttrell to safety.

OPERATION PHANTOM PHOENIX

It was Christmas Eve 2007. Army Rangers in Mosul, Iraq, learned that a terrorist group had held a public execution. People even told the Rangers in which home the terrorists were based.

The Rangers were already in Iraq on a mission. They were to collect information about the terrorists. Whenever possible, they were to capture terrorist leaders. More importantly, they were to stop terrorists from kidnapping and murdering more people. Now the Rangers knew where to find them.

They entered the terrorists' compound at night. "You're always thinking for the worst," said Staff Sergeant Paul Hegleth.[9] Rangers expect to face armed enemies. They expect suicide vests and grenades. Hegleth found

Army Rangers were deployed to Mosul, Iraq, to help protect the Iraqi people from terrorists.

two terrorists using an 11-year-old boy as a human shield. But Hegleth was at the right angle to shoot. He killed both terrorists. The boy was unharmed.

A pair of Rangers saw a strap sticking out underneath a shower. The shower sat on a concrete slab, which concealed a bunker. Terrorists were hidden below the shower where the Rangers could not reach them.

Other terrorists opened fire as Rangers searched the compound. The women and children who lived in the home tried to get out of the line of fire. Sergeant 1st Class Laraun Charles helped each of them over the outer wall to safety. Once this was done, the Rangers called in an Air Force gunship. It shelled the bunker. This was

Sometimes Army Rangers work on missions with other branches of the military, such as the US Air Force.

the end of the last al-Qaeda stronghold in northern Iraq.

The National September 11 Memorial was built to honor the many victims of the 2001 attacks.

FIGHTING THE WAR AGAINST TERRORISM

On December 17, 2020, the Rangers set a record. On that day, the Regiment passed 7,000 days in combat. The counting started after September 11, 2001. That was when nineteen al-Qaeda terrorists hijacked four US airplanes. Two planes were flown into the World Trade Center in New York City. One plane was flown into the Pentagon in Washington, DC.

On the fourth plane, passengers received messages. These messages were from family and friends. They told the passengers about the other crashes. The passengers fought the hijackers. This plane crashed in a field in Pennsylvania. The people on all four planes died. People on the ground also died. A total of nearly 3,000 people were killed.

In October 2001, President George W. Bush made a statement. He said the United States would respond to the attack. It would fight the Global War on Terror.

The Rangers are part of this war. They have conducted missions in Iraq and Afghanistan. Sometimes they have supported the Navy SEALs. Other times they have supported the Army's Delta Force. These joint missions often target high-level terrorists.

Rangers have also led their own missions. They gathered information. They captured targets. They protected important locations. One of these was the Haditha Dam in Iraq. These missions combated terrorism and protected lives.

President George W. Bush announced the invasion of Afghanistan on October 7, 2001. It marked the beginning of the Global War on Terror.

Army Rangers and other US forces protected the Haditha Dam until US Marines returned control of the structure to the Iraqi people in 2008.

Being a Ranger is one of the hardest jobs in the Army. Many of this special force's missions are dangerous. Rangers are known for their bravery, strength, and resourcefulness. This is why they are one of the most respected special forces in the world.

FIRST FEMALE RANGERS

On August 21, 2015, Captain Kristen Griest and 1st Lieutenant Shaye Haver earned their Ranger tabs. They were the first women to graduate from Ranger training. Haver became a helicopter pilot. Griest became a military police platoon leader.

GLOSSARY

ballistic
related to gunfire

fast rope
to slide down a thick rope from a helicopter

hostages
people held against their will by another person, often to exchange for something

infrared
relating to a type of light that is invisible to the human eye but can be seen using special equipment

marksmanship
skill in shooting

post-traumatic stress disorder
a mental and emotional illness caused by trauma

rappelling
descending by sliding down a rope

shrapnel
fragments thrown by an explosion

SOURCE NOTES

CHAPTER ONE: BECOMING AN ARMY RANGER

1. Quoted in Ryan Luke, "What It Means to Be an Army Ranger, According to 7 Rangers," *Coffee or Die*, November 6, 2019. https://coffeeordie.com.

2. Quoted in Luke, "What It Means to Be an Army Ranger, According to 7 Rangers."

3. Lisa Jaster, "Lisa Jaster on Being a Female US Army Ranger," *AFP Conversations*, n.d. www.afponline.org.

CHAPTER TWO: ARMY RANGER EQUIPMENT

4. Quoted in Aj Caldwell, "Every Piece of Gear in a Ranger's Night Raid Bag," *Insider*, May 4, 2023. www.insider.com.

5. Quoted in Caldwell, "Every Piece of Gear in a Ranger's Night Raid Bag."

CHAPTER THREE: THE WORK OF ARMY RANGERS

6. Quoted in Matthew S. Russell, "Wayland Couple's Son Leading Today's Army Rangers," *Michigan Live*, April 13, 2009. www.mlive.com.

7. Quoted in Russell, "Wayland Couple's Son Leading Today's Army Rangers."

CHAPTER FOUR: ARMY RANGER MISSIONS

8. Quoted in Melinda Waldrop, "From the Battlefield to the Classroom," *University of South Carolina*, September 13, 2017. https://sc.edu.

9. Quoted in Patrick R. Jennings, "Ranger Raid in Mosul," *Defense Media Network*, December 10, 2021. www.defensemedianetwork.com.

FOR FURTHER RESEARCH

BOOKS

Tammy Gagne, *Life as a Navy SEAL*. San Diego, CA: BrightPoint Press, 2024.

Ashley Gish, *Army Rangers*. Mankato, MN: Creative Education, 2021.

Howard Phillips, *Inside the Army Rangers*. New York: PowerKids Press, 2022.

INTERNET SOURCES

"The Army Rangers: Mission and History," *Military.com*, n.d. www.military.com.

"Ranger Handbook," *United States Army Infantry School*, April 2000. www.atu.edu.

Jim Tice, "Be an Army Ranger Now: Long List of Job Opportunities," *Army Times*, April 18, 2016. www.armytimes.com.

WEBSITES

Ranger Hall of Fame
https://ranger.org/ranger-hall-of-fame

The Ranger Hall of Fame was formed in 1992. The Hall of Fame preserves the legacy of the very best Rangers.

US Army Rangers
www.army.mil/ranger

The official US Army Ranger website offers information about the 75th Ranger Regiment.

US Army Special Operations Command History Office
https://arsof-history.org/index.html

The US Army Special Operations Command History Office site recounts special forces history. Interested readers will find information on Rangers, commandos, and more.

INDEX

Airborne Rangers, 42
al Qaeda, 51, 53
Armed Services Vocational Aptitude Battery, 12–14
Army Ranger bases, 19
Army Ranger School, 34
awards, 10

Braun, Jacob, 30–31, 33

Church, Thomas R., 42–43
combat engineers, 38–39

drones, 36–38

equipment, 24–33
Eubank, Dave, 17

fast roping, 24, 33
female Rangers, 57
foreign languages, 39

Global War on Terror, 54
Gould, Jesse, 17

handbook, 32
Hegleth, Paul, 48–51
hostages, 7, 8, 9, 10

Islamic State of Iraq and Syria, 7, 8, 9

Jaster, Lisa, 20–22

Laraun, Charles, 50
Luttrell, Marcus, 46–47, 48

marksmanship, 22–23
missions, 6–11, 16, 28–29, 34, 35, 38–39
motto, 10

Operation Phantom Phoenix, 48–51
Operation Red Wings, 44–48

Payne, Thomas "Patrick," 6, 7–8, 9, 10
physical fitness, 14–15

rappelling, 21
requirements, 14–15
retirement, 40–43
Reyes, Mario, 47

September 11 attacks, 53–54
success rate, 22

Taliban, 44–45
training, 14–23, 26, 36, 39, 40, 42, 43, 57

vehicles, 24–26

weapons, 26–28

IMAGE CREDITS

Cover: © Samuel King Jr./US Air Force/DVIDS
5: © Sgt. William Begley/US Army/DVIDS
7: © Spc. Philip Diab/US Army/DVIDS
8: © Petty Officer 1st Class Carlos M. Vazquez II/US DOD/DVIDS
11: © Spc. Wyatt Moore/US Army/DVIDS
13: © Sgt. Christopher Gaylord/US Army/DVIDS
15: © Patrick A. Albright/US Army/DVIDS
16: © Sgt. Richard W. Jones Jr./US Army/DVIDS
19: © Red Line Editorial
21: © Patrick A. Albright/US Army/DVIDS
25: © Sgt. 1st Class Raymond Piper/US Army/DVIDS
27: © Spc. Elizabeth Erste/US Army/DVIDS
29: © Lance Cpl. Colton Brownlee/US Marine Corps/DVIDS
30: © Sgt. Christopher Osburn/US Army Reserve/DVIDS
35: © Patrick A. Albright/US Army/DVIDS
37: © Airman 1st Class Madeline Baisey/US Air Force/DVIDS
38: © Staff Sgt. Arturo Guzman/US Army/DVIDS
41: © Capt. Charles An/US Army/DVIDS
45: © Sgt. 1st Class Adam Stone/US Army/DVIDS
47: © US Navy/DVIDS
49: © Defense Imagery Management Operations Center/DVIDS
51: © Senior Airman Amanda A. Flower-Raschella/US Air Force/DVIDS
52: © anderm/Shutterstock Images
55: © Eric Draper/George W. Bush Presidential Library/American Photo Archive/Alamy
56: © Cpl. Tyler Hill/US Navy/DVIDS

ABOUT THE AUTHOR

Sue Bradford Edwards is a nonfiction author. She lives and works in Saint Louis, Missouri, where she has written more than forty books for young readers. Her BrightPoint books include *Become a Construction Equipment Operator*, *What Are Learning Disorders?*, *Robotics in Health Care*, and *Being Black in America*. Her father was in the Air Force. She grew up hearing about the brave men and women who serve in the US military.